Deer

Written by Alex Hall

From Head to Hoof

Enslow PUBLISHING

Published in 2025 by Enslow Publishing, LLC
2544 Clinton Street
Buffalo, NY 14224

Written by:
Alex Hall

Edited by:
Rebecca Phillips-Bartlett

Designed by:
Jasmine Pointer

Cataloging-in-Publication Data
Names: Hall, Alex.
Title: Deer / Alex Hall.
Description: Buffalo, NY : Enslow Publishing, 2025. | Series: From head to hoof | Includes glossary.
Identifiers: ISBN 9781978541924 (pbk.) | ISBN 9781978541931 (library bound) | ISBN 9781978541948 (ebook)
Subjects: LCSH: Deer--Juvenile literature. | Deer--Anatomy--Juvenile literature. | Deer--Behavior--Juvenile literature. | Deer--Life cycles--Juvenile literature.
Classification: LCC QL737.U55 H355 2025 | DDC 599.65--dc23

Manufactured in the United States of America

CPSIA compliance information: Batch #CW25ENS: For further information contact Enslow Publishing LLC at 1-800-398-2504.

Image Credits

All images are courtesy of Shutterstock.com. With thanks to Getty Images, Thinkstock Photo and iStockphoto.

Cover – ARTvektor, Lindylouwho, Tony Campbell, Vector Tradition. Throughout – Deka Vision. 2–3 – Giedriius. 4–5 – David Osborn, Hugh Lansdown, Tom Reichner. 6–7 – Dmitry Chulov, Jamie Hall. 8–9 – Ben Wehrman, designerpunk. 10–11 – marcin jucha, Danny Ye. 12–13 – Budimir Jevtic, Foonia. 14–15 – Giedriius, Tom Reichner, David G Hayes. 16–17 – Dennis Jacobsen, Pictureguy, Cynthia Vannoy. 18–19 – WildMedia, Steve Oehlenschlager. 20–21 – Lindylouwho, boybehindacamera. 22–23 – Tony Campbell, L-N.

Contents

Words that look like <u>this</u> can be found in the glossary on page 24.

Deer

From massive moose to little muntjacs, there are over 40 species of deer in the world. Most deer live in woodlands and marshes. The place an animal or plant lives is called its habitat.

Moose

Muntjac

It is time to look at all the amazing parts that make deer interesting mammals. So, let's explore the bodies of a deer, from the top of their heads to the bottom of their hooves.

Head

Most deer have antlers at the top of their heads. Antlers are made of bone. Mostly only male deer have antlers. Female reindeer are the only female deer with antlers.

A female deer is called a doe.

Male deer are called bucks or stags.

Male deer use their antlers to fight. They fight by locking their antlers together. Male deer usually fight during mating season so they can mate with a doe.

Eyes

Deer have eyes on the sides of their heads. This allows them to see more of their surroundings and look out for danger. This helps them protect themselves from predators.

People once thought that deer were colorblind. However, we now know they can see some colors better than humans can. Deer do not have good eyesight during the day, but they can see well at night.

Mouth

Deer do not have top front teeth. Instead, they have something called a dental pad. The dental pad helps them eat grass and young plants. Most deer are herbivores. This means they only eat plants.

Some deer might eat meat if they cannot find plants.

A few species of deer have fang-like teeth. Chinese water deer bucks use these teeth to fight instead of growing antlers. They can even pull their teeth back into their mouths to eat.

Nose

Deer have small noses and a good sense of smell. A deer's powerful sense of smell is a lot better than a human's. Deer can often smell danger before they can see it.

Deer have many ways of communicating with other deer. They make loud snorts and grunts by blowing air out of their nostrils. This makes a loud noise that can be heard from far away.

Body

Deer have fur coats that keep their bodies warm. Their coats have two layers. This helps them stay warm while in the water. Many deer have brown coats to help them camouflage in woodlands.

Deer's coats change throughout the year to cope with changes to weather. Their lighter-colored coats help them stay cool in the summer. Darker-colored coats help them stay warm in the winter.

Tail

Not all deer have the same size tails. Sika deer have short tails with a black stripe. The white-tailed deer is named after its long, white-patterned tail.

When deer see danger, they point their tails up. This warns other deer about the danger. This is called flagging. White tails also help baby deer follow their mothers through thick, dark woodlands.

Legs

Deer have thin legs that help them run fast. This helps deer escape predators and find somewhere to hide. Deer that live in places where they cannot hide easily are even faster runners.

Deer's strong legs help them jump high. The white-tailed deer is known for its leaping. It can jump up to 9 feet (3 m) high. That is higher than the height of a room in a house.

Hooves

Deer have hooves at the bottom of their legs. Hooves are made of keratin, which is the same thing human nails are made of. Deer have two small and two large hooves on each foot.

All animals with hooves are called ungulates.

Deer hooves are strong. The strength of their hooves helps them turn quickly while running. Deer also use their hooves to push off the ground when they jump.

Life Cycle

A baby deer is called a fawn. A doe can give birth to three fawns at a time. Fawns do not have a strong smell. This makes it harder for predators to find them.

Life cycles are the changes living things go through during their lives, leading up to being able to have their own young.

Fewer plants grow in the winter, which means there is less food for deer. They spend most of the winter resting to save energy. Most deer live for around three to six years.

Glossary

camouflage to blend in with the surroundings

communicating passing information between two or more things

energy the power that makes living things able to move and live

female the sex that can produce offspring or eggs

give birth when a mother creates a baby from her body

male the sex that fathers offspring

mammals animals that are warm-blooded, have a backbone, and produce milk to feed their children

mating season the time of year when an animal looks for a partner of the same species to create young with

predators animals that hunt other animals for food

species a group of very similar animals or plants that can create young together

Index